P9-DTK-344

The Meaning of Health
The Relation of Religion and Health

The Meaning of Health

The Relation of Religion and Health

Paul Tillich

Edited & Introduction by Paul Lee

North Atlantic Books Richmond California

ISBN 0-913028-81-9 (paperback)
ISBN 0-913028-87-8 (cloth)

Publishers:

North Atlantic Books
635 Amador Street
Richmond, California 94805

Platonic Academy
P.O. Box 409
Santa Cruz, California 95061

Contents

Introduction   7

The Relation of Religion and Health   13

The Meaning of Health   51

Introduction

The depiction of Hygieia in the mural devoted to medicine at the University of Vienna, by Gustav Klimt, expresses the artistic and cultural background that formed Paul Tillich as a German philosopher and theologian. Vienna was the center for the "*fin-de-siècle*," as well as the center for many of the prophetic visions and movements of the century to come, expressed in the Viennese novelists and satirists Karl Kraus, Musil, Kafka, Brock, Von Dodderer. Freud discovered psychoanalysis there, when, as a latter-day Heraclitus, he searched for himself, like a deep-sea diver, and began the process of self- and other-analysis, which, along with Existentialism and Expressionism, became the form-breaking powers of the 20th century.

As the daughter of Asclepias, Hygieia is the bearer of healing power, particularly in her priestess and hieratic pose in Klimt's rendering. Bearing snakes, the ancient symbol of the convergence of poison and medicine (where dosage determines the difference), Hygieia heralds "the unity of life and death, the interpenetration of instinctual vitality and personal dissolution." (Schorske).

The snakes of Asclepias, wound on the the staff, the caduceus, were said to come out at night and lick the wounds of those who came to sleep in the temples in a practice known as "incubation," where the God would appear in a dream omen announcing the prospects for a cure.

In his comprehensive discussion of Western modes of healing, Tillich mentions how Asclepias vied with the Christ as the preeminent bearer of healing — the Great Physician of the ancient world.

When I was a young graduate student at Union Theological Seminary, I heard Tillich deliver the Bampton Lectures at Columbia University — BIBLICAL RELIGION AND THE SEARCH FOR ULTIMATE REALITY, where he overcame the Humpty-

Dumpty problem in Western religion by putting the two cultures together again in all of their dialectical tension — Athens and Jerusalem. While at Union, I discovered the essay — THE RELATION OF RELIGION AND HEALTH — and copied it out longhand.

As the son of a doctor, I had decided against medicine and for theology and philosophy as a career. Tillich restored to me the lost unity of these two subject matters, as well, by placing the theme of 'healing' and the meaning of health in its old cosmic frame, within the context of salvation and its etymological origins. Healing is restored to its religious dignity. Tillich shows this ancient unity of powers and functions before their historical separation. He anticipated the longing for their mutual convergence as currently expressed in the Wholistic Health Movement now sweeping the country in all of its varied forms.

As a thinker on the boundary line, Tillich was able to negotiate territory neglected by others who remained bound to the confines of their own viewpoints and specialties. He was able to show the deep associations between otherwise seemingly separated fields. Therefore, the current split between industrial medicine and traditional medicine, as practiced worldwide in non-industrial nations, as well as ethnic groups in rural areas everywhere, is an unfortunate consequence of a trend of a century and a half. When biochemistry isolated the active ingredients of natural medicine to synthesize artificially from inorganic sources, biochemistry undermined the botanical foundation of medicine. Tillich's discussion reviews the long historic development and sets the stage for re-evaluating the contribution of neglected and rejected styles in the healing arts burdened by their association with religion and a vitalist approach to health and disease.

In THE RELATION OF RELIGION AND HEALTH, Tillich sketches out the background for what he carried through in THE COURAGE TO BE. I have come to call it "The *Thymós* Doctrine," the old Homeric word Tillich translated as "the courage to be." When I found out that the word for the herb — thyme — and for the gland — thymus — were cognates, *thymós* became the theme for my life's work.

In my judgement, Tillich anticipated the development of modern immunology in THE COURAGE TO BE. Once one follows through the meaning of '*thymós*' in the discovery of the thymus and the central role of the thymus in immunology, as well as the classic herb — thyme — in the rediscovery of the healing properties of herbs and the significance of traditional or herbal medicine worldwide, THE COURAGE TO BE is seen as an essay in theological and philosophical immunology, a discourse on the vital dynamics of self-affirmation in the face of all that would undo and destroy us, where our constitutional defense is called into play, otherwise known as our immune system. Tillich gives us a spiritual biology of the immune system, where THE COURAGE TO BE is our thymic vigour.

After reading in the field of immunology for the last ten years, it is possible to mount a new argument for the existence of God based on the *infinite* diversity of antibody response to antigens (*anti*-body *gen*-erating). As though to fulfill the vision of Leibnitz that we live in the 'best of all possible worlds,' immunology is now discovering that we have the best of all possible immune systems.

With his unerring facility for language and theoretical formulation, Tillich picked just the right word for his pursuit of the meaning of health and the relation of religion and health begun here in these two essays as the background for THE COURAGE TO BE.

The Thymós Doctrine is sketched out here in his effort to construct a theoretical model of the human self for the purpose of determining a complex of relations necessary for any discussion of the meaning of health. This model, although the term '*thymós*' is not mentioned, should be read as the theoretical background for the subsequent elucidation. To read these two essays as a preparation for THE COURAGE TO BE provides the student of health with a rich historical and theoretical background.

It is appropriate to introduce this material into the current discussion for the sake of supporting the quest for models of wholeness that overcome the bifurcation of the healing arts into technical specialties with everyone lost in their own niche. It is time for the left hand to know what the right hand is doing.

To think through the cultural modalities of the healing arts in order to restore the full dimensions of human health is the task we all share in this late stage of the self-destruction of industrial

9

society. Tillich points the way, as he tried to do in everything he thought and wrote, as one of the great fighters against the demonic 'structures of destruction' that would destroy life as we know it on this earth, whether through synthetic simulation or radiation and pollution.

Healing, again, can become a religious vocation, when the medical arts and sciences join with the priest and the prophet, the curendero and native healer, in the mutual acknowledgement of converging domains, where wholeness is the consequence of a new "planet medicine."

This "planet medicine" is the avowed goal of the WORLD HEALTH ORGANIZATION. In 1978, upon the successful completion of the campaign to rid the world of smallpox, Dr. Halfdan Mahler, the Director-General, announced the goal for the year 2000 — "Health For All" — through the promotion and advancement of traditional medicine worldwide.

For someone like myself, a student of Tillich's, and a spokesman for the medicinal herb renaissance in America, this goal strikes me as the basis for one of the most creative and promising dialogues of the next two decades. When I met a second year Stanford Medical School student — a native American Indian — who told me about his initiation into the herbal medicine of his tribe, I thought I had encountered the best example of the new 'cross-fertilization of cultures,' which the dialogue between traditional, basically herbal, medicine and modern industrial medicine entails.

In such figures, we may hope to see the confluence of themes and trends, styles and models of medicine and health, developed in different times and in various climes, brought together, for the benefit of all. In this way, the healing arts and sciences and their history, so richly reviewed here with all of their problems and complexities brought to light, may contribute again to the history of salvation.

Paul Lee
Santa Cruz, California

BIBLIOGRAPHY

FIN-DE-SIÈCLE, by Carl Schorske, Random House, 1981.

HYGIEIA, A Woman's Herbal, by Jeannine Parvat, Freestone Collective, 1978.

ASCLEPIAS, by Karl Kerenyi, Bollingen Books, Princeton University Press.

IDENTITY AND THE LIFE CYCLE, by Erik Erikson, Psychological Issues I,1, International Universities Press, New York, 1979

"Wholeness and Totality," in TOTALITARIANISM, C. J. Friedrich, ed., Harvard University Press, 1954.

THE BIOLOGY OF ULTIMATE CONCERN, by Theodosius Dobzhansky, New American Library, New York, 1967.

PLANET MEDICINE, by Richard Grossinger, Doubleday Anchor, New York, 1980.

THE DOUBLE FACE OF JANUS and Other Essays in the History of Medicine, by Owsei Temkin, The Johns Hopkins University Press, Baltimore, 1978.

THE COURAGE TO BE, by Paul Tillich, Yale University Press, New Haven, 1952.

THE METAPHORS OF CONSCIOUSNESS, ed. by Ronald S. Valle and Rolf von Eckartsberg, Chap. 25, "Thymós as Biopsychological Metaphor: The Vital Root of Consciousness," by Paul Lee, Plenum Press, New York, 1981.

The Relation of Religion and Health

The unity of salvation and healing as presented in religious myth

The word "RELIGION" is not a religious word, but a term designating a special realm of human behavior, as seen from the point of view of an observer. It is natural that this concept of religion is used in a modern academic enterprise, and that the relation of the religious realm to other realms should be under inquiry and discussion. Religion itself, however, does not talk about religion, but about God, the world, and the soul.

I do not intend to devaluate the observer's point of view, but heeding the warning myself, I wish to start by directing attention to some old classical ideas about the relationship of religion and health. And in doing so we must leave the outside view and identify outselves with the inside view. We must replace "religion" by "salvation," and must ask: What is the place of health in the frame of the idea of salvation?

In asking this question, we do not turn to the modern theological doctrines of salvation for an answer. They have mostly lost the original power of the idea of salvation, its cosmic meaning which includes nature, man as a whole, and society. Especially in modern Protestantism, salvation, and many related concepts such as regeneration, redemption, eternal life, are interpreted as descriptions of the spiritual situation of the individual man, in which a special stress is laid on his moral transformation and the continuation of his personal life after death. But for biblical and early Christian thinking, salvation is basically a cosmic event: the *world* is saved. The same is equally true for religious thinking generally in the cults and myths immediately preceding and surrounding early Christianity. This whole age used the same words and carried their cosmic connotations into the feeling and thinking of the Church. But we should enlarge our horizons still further, because in the primitive, as well as the high religions of

13

mankind, we find this cosmic reference in the idea of salvation, not always equally strong, but almost never missing.

When salvation has cosmic significance, healing is not only included in it, but *salvation can be described as the act of "cosmic healing."* The root of the word "salvation" in many languages indicates this. Thus, the Greek word *soteria* is derived from *saos*; the Latin word *salvatio* from *salvus*; the German word *Heiland* from *heil*, which is akin to the English word "healing." *Saos, salvus, heil,* mean whole, not yet split, not disrupted, not disintegrated, and therefore healthy and sane. In Matthew 9:22, the English translation of *sesoken se* ("he saved thee," referring to an act of healing by Jesus) reads: "made thee whole." Salvation is basically and essentially healing, the re-establishment of a whole that was broken, disrupted, disintegrated.

Moreover, mythological vision agrees with philology that not only man (body and soul) but also nature, or more exactly the universe, is sick and needs healing, and will be healed in the event of salvation. Thus, in sections of the Indian *Mahābhārata* the *kālīyuga* is described as the last, most disintegrated period of a cosmic eon. In it nature is sick, the vital powers of birth and growth have deteriorated in all living beings, plants, animals, and men. Consequently incurable sickness and early death prevail. Quite similarly, Isa. 24:4 and II Esdras (both of them late apocalyptic writings) speak of the fading away of the earth and the degeneration of all natural forces. So, too, the Apocalypses of Mark and of John describe the disintegration of the astronomic cosmos and the plagues on earth before the final salvation. A symptom of the cosmic disorder is the enmity between different parts of nature and between man and nature. The order of nature, called "covenant" between God and "the beasts of the field" (Hos. 2:18), is broken, and the result is chaos and self-destruction. Psalm 90, in its oldest part, complains in unison with many pagan witnesses of the laborious life and early death of man, explaining it by the breach beween God and man, thus echoing the old myth of paradise lost in the fall. The land itself fell sick, and produces weeds under the curse of God, which results in enmity between man and animals (represented by the serpent), extreme pain in childbirth, fratricide, and, above all, in the loss of the food of the gods (the fruits of the tree of life) which

14

in paradise continually overcame the natural mortality of man.

Not much citation is needed to prove that the idea of salvation, in the sense of making whole or healing, is applied to the social disruption of mankind as much as to cosmic disintegration. The patriarchal power of man over woman, the division of languages, the cleavage between nomadic and agricultural forms of existence, the rise of world powers and tyrants, the national wars which become more and more destructive: all this is the state of society which needs the healer and the universally saving event. But most interesting and important for the relation — more exactly the identity — between healing and salvation is the mythological interpretation of the psychic disruptions in man, or in other beings in which psychic forces are presupposed. These disruptions are the effect of "demonic powers" which take "possession" of the soul. The mentally ill are the possessed, but not only they. Many bodily diseases are derived from this source. And social evils, especially idolatrous tyrants, false prophets and messiahs, pagan empires and religions, are the work of demons. So are most of the natural evils. They are especially powerful when the world becomes old, loses its vitality and its power of resistance against idolatry and crime, hate and self-destruction, bodily and mental disease. Nature, society, and soul are subject to the same principle of disintegration. They all are possessed by demons, or, as we should say, by psychic forces of destruction.

But this possession by forces of evil is not a natural event. It is the result of a divine curse which itself is the result of "sin," i.e., of an act of separation, of rebellion in which the responsible ego participates, and which involves guilt. *The cosmic disease is cosmic guilt.* No one is excepted from this guilt. A universal feeling is justified, and so is the feeling of guilt in connection with natural, social, bodily, and mental diseases. On the other hand, the universal character of disease and evil makes it impossible to derive them in a special case from a special act. All higher religions have fought against such calculating moralism with respect to disease and guilt; most significantly, The Book of Job and The Fourth Gospel. Disease and guilt are no less a matter of personal responsibility because they are cosmic, but they are not a matter of proportional calculation, just *because* they are cosmic and precede every individual act.

15

The myths of salvation correspond strictly to the myths of cosmic disease. This can be shown point by point: the disintegration of nature is overcome in salvation, the act of cosmic healing. A new earth, an everlasting spring (i.e., a vitality of the cosmos which never declines), a renewal of paradise is envisaged. The "garden" is the place where the curse upon the land is overcome. In it vegetative nature is liberated from chaos and self-destruction; "weed" there is none. This "garden of the gods," of which every human garden is a symbol and an anticipation, will reappear in the salvation of nature. Peace is re-established in nature (Isa. 11:6), a new covenant is made with the beasts of the fields (Hos. 2:18). The wild nature in animals, as well as in nations and human individuals, is overcome by shepherd-kings such as Orpheus, Poimandres, David, and Jesus. Saints live with and preach to animals, for they "are not excluded from the knowledge of God." (Clement Alex. *Stromata*, V, 13)

Bodily health is re-established. "Health shall descend and sickness shall be removed," says the Apocalypse of Baruch, in the new aeon. In Greece and later Hellenism, Asclepius, the deified master of healing, is one of the earliest gods to be called *theoi soteres* (savior gods). He is one of the most significant figures in the later Hermetic mysteries of salvation. The identity of healing and salvation is nowhere clearer than in Asclepius, except perhaps in Jesus of Nazareth. This is the reason why Origen and his pagan adversary, Celsus, dispute as to the higher medical quality of Jesus or of Asclepius. In the Gospel of Mark, Jesus is, first of all, the healer, because the coming of the Kingdom of God implies the appearance of an irresistable healing power. When John the Baptist, from his prison, sends his disciples to ask Jesus if he is the Messiah, Jesus answers in the affirmative by pointing to his healing power. The blind receive their sight and the lame walk, the lepers are cleansed and the deaf hear, and the dead are raised up and the poor have good tidings preached to them (Matt. 11:5). This is the new aeon: bodily and social diseases are overcome, and death is conquered. The same power is given to the apostles who announce that salvation has come. "And he called unto him his twelve disciples and gave them authority over unclean spirits, to cast them out, and to heal all manner of disease and all manner of sickness" (Matt. 10). And a few verses later,

16

Jesus says to them: "And as ye go, preach, saying the kingdom of heaven is at hand. Heal the sick, raise the dead, cleanse the lepers, cast out demons." The identity of healing, bodily and mental, and the presence of salvation can not be expressed more clearly. To announce that salvation is at hand and to heal is one and the same act. To perform both parts of this act is the task of the disciples — this and nothing else.

In the social realm the healers of the body-politic are called *soteres*, saviors. Thus the successors of Alexander the Great, Augustus as the bringer of peace, and the kings of Israel, above all the expected Messiah, are "saviors." Isis is called savior because she heals the disorder among men as well as among the stars. Zoroaster calls himself the "healer of life" brought into disorder by the demonic devas. In the eschatological visions of The Book of Revelations, the leaves of the tree of life — which reappears in the future fulfillment — serve the "healing of the nations."

Salvation or cosmic healing is dependent upon victory over the demonic forces. According to the picture of Jesus that we have in the Synoptics, his messianic vocation was confirmed for himself by his power over the demonic realm. The story of his temptation, the vision of Satan falling from heaven like lightning, and, above all, the healing of the demoniacs, these are all evaluated as signs of the salvation which has arrived. "If I by the Spirit of God cast out demons then is the Kingdom of God come upon you" (Matt. 12:26). Grace (another word for the Spirit of God) conquers "possession." Thus, the healing of mental illness is the most crucial proof of salvation, although mental diseases are not separated off from bodily and social diseases in the accounts.

Healing in the sense of salvation includes the conquest of death. In many myths death is, on the one hand, the consequence of cosmic disease and guilt. On the other hand, it is the fulfillment of the law of finitude. In the latter sense it is natural: "from dust to dust" (Genesis), from the "infinite" (*apeiron*) to the "infinite" (Anaximander). In the former sense it is unnatural, as is the whole cosmic disease, and is overcome in salvation. Salvation is the presence of Eternal Life, which is a state of things into which one "enters," or which one "inherits" and "takes in possession." The clearest expression of the connection between disease and death, on the other hand, and salvation and eternal life (*not* to be confused with physical immortality), on the other hand, is the famous description of the sacramental food as a *pharmakon athanasias*, a medicine which heals from death, and overcomes exclusion from the realm of eternity.

Cosmic disease is cosmic guilt. Salvation, therefore, is the conquest of guilt and its cause, wilful separation or sin. The decisive sign of this aspect of salvation is reconciliation, the re-establishment of a unity which was lost and transformed into enmity. Reconciliation on the part of the gods, whose wrath correlates with the feeling of guilt, is sought in most religions. The way is the ritual sacrifice which appeases the divine wrath and removes the feeling of guilt. The self-negation which is implied in every sacrifice accepts *and* overcomes the divine negation of the self. In many mystery religions, and in Christianity, not god but man is won over, reconciled. The god offers himself as a sacrifice. This acceptance is faith, which means an ecstatic self-transcending act in which man is reconciled with the god and with himself. The guilt consciousness of the unreconciled stage is conquered, and with it the special form of anxiety of death in the sense of unnatural exclusion from eternity is overcome. In this way the deepest implications of the cosmic disease in which man participates are healed: guilt, anxiety, fear of death. This is the function of reconciliation, to make whole the man who struggles against himself. It reaches the center of personality, and unites man not only with his god and with himself, but also with other men and with nature. Reconciliation in the center of personality results in a reconciliation in all directions, and he who is reconciled is able to love. Salvation is the healing of the cosmic disease which prevents love.

The savior is the healer. Jesus calls himself a physician. The power of the saviors is based on their cosmic significance, that is, on the fact that they represent the whole which they are supposed to bring back to its lost wholeness. This implies that they are divine and cosmic figures, divine, implying centralized unity and indestructible control over themselves and things, cosmic, implying their all-embracing universality. Yet the saviors are also human, because in man the cosmos is united and healed. The savior is the "man from above," the "heavenly man," the "son of man," the god "anthropos," the "god-man," etc. He is the concentration of all cosmic powers, the macrocosmos condensed in a mi-

18

crocosmos. The microcosmos-idea, so important in the history of healing, is a savior-idea and not a theoretical analogy between man and world. Man is able to mediate between the different strata of reality, because they are all in him. He can know them and he can transform them. In the early Renaissance, when the mythological heritage of the ancient world was revived and slowly transformed into modern science, the savior function or healing role of man is powerfully expressed. At first it is still described in mythological terms: the savior-man is the Christ, the God-man. Then it is generalized: the savior-man is the rational, the microcosmic man. At first it is still magic, astrological, alchemic practice which makes him the cosmic healer; then it is technical, astronomic, chemical insights which give him the healing power. At first the psychic realm is decisive, then body and mind became separated from the psychic ground and isolated over against each other. When this separation takes place, myth is replaced by science, and the identity of salvation and healing is broken. Both of them lose their cosmic character, salvation becomes concerned with the individual soul, healing with the individual body.

The means of salvation or cosmic healing is primarily the divine act in which the demonic forces are overcome and cosmic disorder brought to a new order. In it the healing power appears on "earth" as an individual life, and is tested by suffering and death in its divine wholeness; institutions of salvation are established, and a final fulfillment is promised and prepared. Secondly, salvation or cosmic healing becomes actual in the human activities through which individuals participate in the power of salvation or the universal process of healing. The cult is supposed to effect this by introducing man into the sources of salvation, or by introducing the powers of healing into the particular individual or social situation. The priest is the mediator between the objective reality of salvation and the subjective appropriation of it. Through the priest (who is always and essentially a "medicine-man"), the cosmic wholeness which is effected by the saving act of God becomes the power of individual or social wholeness. Holy words, incantations, charms, and sacramental objective acts, are different tools of his mediation. Salvation or healing occurs *modo participationis*, by participation, namely, in something objective which precedes any special act of saving or healing. He who has the healing power does not have it from himself, but from a special transmission of the universal healing power unto him. The healing power is rooted in the divine realm. Only the power which controls the cosmic wholeness is able to create individual wholeness. The divine beings as representatives of the power which carries the cosmos are the saviors and original healers, e.g., the mystery and mediator gods. Union with them is the means of salvation or healing, whether performed by magic influence or by mystical identification, by moral obedience or by self-transcending faith.

Three theological considerations may conclude this prelude in the key of classical myth. First, it is obvious that, as long as the idea of cosmic salvation or healing is acceped, bodily, mental, and spiritual healing are not separated. For all elements of reality belong to the cosmic wholeness. All levels of being are disintegrated by the disruption of this wholeness, and are reintegrated by the basic act and permanent process of cosmic healing.

Secondly, it must be pointed out that healing, in this mythological atmosphere, has not the character of a miracle in the rationalistic sense of the term, even though a god or messiah is the healer. For the presence of the cosmic power of salvation in special persons and acts, which are "signs" of its universal presence, is not the suspension of natural laws, as a misguided supernaturalism asserts. This very rationalistic irrationalism should be dismissed like any other superstition. Genuine religion never has used such a concept, and serious theology should not even ponder it. As Dawson says: "There is no violation of the laws of nature.... The divine and spiritual power is here already waiting to be used."[1]

Thirdly, how is the relation to be understood that myth declares between individual acts of salvation or healing and the cosmic act? I suggest that this relation be designated as a fragmentary, ambiguous, anticipatory realization of the cosmic wholeness. Each of these terms carries some special connotations. "Fragmentary" indicates the fact that every specific state of health or salvation represents the cosmic wholeness in a being which is a fragment of the whole, and whose wholeness is, therefore, always conditioned, threatened, imperfect, and pointing be-

20

yond itself. "Ambiguous" indicates the fact that, from the point of view of the whole, all partial healing is doubtful in its ultimate value. The saving of one limb may be the cause for a disintegration of a whole personality. Moral health may be the cause for the diseases of phariseeism. "Anticipatory" indicates the preliminary character of healing and salvation in comparison with the eschatological fulfillment for which many religions are longing. Anticipation unites an already with a not yet, and this is the attitude in which salvation or healing must be experienced in the world of the classic myths.

Against the identification of salvation and healing it has been said, for instance by Hiltner,[2] that healing has temporal, while salvation has eternal reference, even when the object of healing is body, mind, and spirit. But this argument is based on a modern, Protestant definition of both concepts. It implies a conscious or unconscious rejection of the idea of cosmic disease, the universal fall, and of cosmic healing, the universal redemption. It does not see that the eternal fulfillment is actual in the fragmentary fulfillment in time and space. Healing as well as salvation are temporal and, at the same time, are eternal. Healing acquires the significance of the eternal, and salvation the actuality of the temporal. From this point of view, it becomes impossible for the physician to relegate salvation to a fantastic realm of the eternal, and likewise impossible for the minister to deprive the physician's work, even when religion is not explicitly used in it, of its absolute seriousness.

Religious, magic, and natural healing distinguished

Their distinction and confusion in ancient and modern souces.
From earliest times to the present, three ways of healing are recognized in the source literature: religious or spiritual healing, magic or psychic healing, and bodily or natural healing. Each of these concepts is not only vague in itself, but there is a continuous confusion and overlapping of them, and, still more striking, a permanent attempt on the part of each to swallow up the others. Examples for the distinction as well as the confusion of the three ways of healing are abundant in both ancient and modern times.

21

The Assyrians and Babylonians distinguished, without separating them however, the religious element in healing, which consisted for them in sacrifice and prayer directed towards beings of a superhuman character, the magic element, consisting in mutual sympathetic influence between human and cosmic forces, and the natural element, consisting in drugs or the knife. The Persians distinguished the "word-doctor" from the "herb-doctor" and the "knife-doctor." About the first, they said: "This one is the best of all healers who deals with the Holy Word, and he will drive away sickness from the body of the faithful."[3] The Holy Word, here, is obviously a religious word with magic power, showing the mixture of religion and magic in a form which always remained very important: the *word*. (The Persians gave us the term "magic.") But Origen, also, says: "It is not the thing signified, but the qualities and peculiarities of words which possess a certain power for this or that purpose." Therefore, he asserts, no other word should be used for God than the word God, and no other spiritual healing is possible than through the use of the name, Jesus Christ. What is religious, what is magic in this kind of healing?

Jumping to the present, we find the distinction of the three ways of healing precisely expressed by Hiltner when he says:

In some cases the surgeons must cut out offending tissue in order to release the forces of healing, in other cases personality analysis is the central need, and in still other cases conscious recognition of the divine power of the healing influences is most needed. In the majority of cases, something of all three may be helpful. We know more about when the surgeon's knife or a drug or a new diet is needed, than we know about the others. We know more about when personality analysis is needed than we do about when prayer is needed.[4]

This sounds not very different from the old Persian text, except that they knew more about the herb and word medicine than about the knife. But again we must ask: what is the relation of the realms presupposed by the three ways of healing? What is religious, and what is psychic?

The mixture of the three in a religious formulary is illustrated

22

in the old Christian Sacramentary of Serapion, where the following prayer accompanies the unction of the sick:

We pray Thee send out a healing power of the only-begotten from heaven upon this oil, that it may become to those who are being anointed with it, for a throwing off of every disease and infirmity, for a protection against every demon, for a removal of every unclean spirit, for a driving out of all fever and shivering fit, for good grace and remission of sins, for a medicine of life and salvation.[5]

Here demons, fever, and sins are united, and the healing power from heaven is to be united with the sacred oil. The religious, the psychic, and the natural are completely mixed. Is there a distinction? The same mixture appears in a tractate of Paracelsus concerning the Lord's Supper,[6] where, however, the approach is from the side of the natural elements in healing. For Paracelsus, bread and wine are natural powers, yet sacred by nature's divine character of growth, *before* they enter the sacrament. Again, the natural, the magical, and the religious are also united, when he says: "The true religion of the physician is that he first of all knows and understands all nature in its growth, the inner character of each,"[7] and about the inner character, he adds: "Therefore, he is a philosopher, who if he knows something in one thing, knows the same also in another thing."[8] This last is magic knowledge, yet for Paracelsus it is, at the same time, philosophy of nature and religion. Is there any way of clearing up these confusions and overlappings?

It can not be denied that religious healing, in the strict sense of the word, was united with magical and natural healing everywhere in the ancient world. The great physicians of the legendary past were deified: Imhotep in Egypt, Asclepius in Greece, Thrita in Persia, etc. Moreover, the centers of healing power were medical temples, such as those of Isis, Asclepius, and, later, certain Christian churches, such as SS. Cosma e Damiani in Rome. The physicians were the priests, or rather the priests were physicians, for the religious aspect did not preclude the use of drugs, medicinal springs, diet, and even surgery. But more important was the magical side, and this in pagan and Christian temple-resorts alike. The practice of incubation, or sleeping in the sacred precinct, during which the healing god appears in a vision for which the patient has been psychologically prepared, shows a typical admixture of magic and religion. The same appears in the use of votive offerings, talismans, incantations, name-magic, etc. in the process of healing. Both empirical medicine and real psychological insight were developed in connection with these practices.

I want to suggest definitions of the religious, the magical, and the natural way of healing, in order to disentangle some of these age-old confusions without doing violence to the complexity of the situation. Indeed, I want to show also why the theoretically clear distinctions are so difficult of application to reality. That the confusions persist in contemporary thinking is very plain. Thus, Dawson writes: "Healing in all its branches has always been ... a process requiring the combination of scientific and religious factors."[9] To prove this he cites, for example, the "faith-healing of witch doctors. But this is just the question, whether such magical healing can be called real "faith-healing," instead of healing by suggestion, and whether it should not be sharply distinguished from religious healing as healing in a genuine state of faith. A battle with magic weapons between two "ghost-shooters" for the life of a man can hardly be called a religious battle, it seems to me, or the suggestive power of such combatants a religious influence. There may be more of a numinous experience involved when the illness is due to the infraction of a taboo, and the healing to a magic reconciliation with the guardians of the taboo. Yet the substance of the event here too is magical and not religious, even though religious feelings may accompany it. Again, it is natural and not religious healing that Herophilus has in mind when he says that medical drugs are the hands of the gods, although the accompanying interpretation is expressed in religious terms. We may compare this with a statement of Hiltner's today, which says: "All healing comes from the *vis medicatrix naturae* or the *vis medicatrix Dei*, the healing power of nature or of God, depending upon whether we are making an empirical or a religious statement."[10] But to derive magical and scientific healing from the Ultimate is not to produce a case of religious healing. And a religious statement about healing is not, ipso facto, a statement about religious healing.

24

Before proceeding to our work of distinction, it may be well to add just a word of reminder as to the gravity of the problem. Thus, from the side of psychiatry, Zilboorg writes: "The union of religion and psychology is a very old phenomenon, and it was destined to play a critical and almost fatal role in the history of psychiatry."[11] Its consequence was "The fusion of insanity, witchcraft, and heresy into one concept."[12] But there is also an opposite danger, namely to lose sight of the psychic in the bodily, as happened in the school of the "brain-mythologists." As Zilboorg puts it: "Medicine captured psychiatry, brought it into its scientific empire, and offered it rights of citizenship only on the condition that it learn the language and submit to the administration ... [but] any appearance of psychology was considered an intrusion or an illegal importation."[13] In our own words, the history is this: Empirical medicine slowly became independent and cut off from religion, while for a time the psychic realm was taken over by religion. At last after its very late liberation from religion, it was taken over by its liberator, empirical medicine, so that now a second liberation has become necessary.

The distinction between magic and religion,
suggestion and faith.
We make a sharp distinction between magic and religion. Magic is "a universal attitude toward the universe."[14] It was primitive man's philosophy. It was his attitude toward nature. Everybody was a magician."[15] Magic was not only theory, however, it was also a technical method of dealing with natural objects, including men. It was a world-view, not a religion. Magic healing is in itself no more religious than physical healing; it is an art, a technique, presupposing a theory about the causes of illness.

The essence of this theory of magic can be described as *the belief in a sympathetic interdependence of all parts of the universe.* This definition, of course, presupposes a high degree of abstraction, and did not appear before the development of rational philosophy. But the existence of the belief itself is as old as the known history of mankind. The definition is derived from the world-view of the later Stoics, for instance, Poseidonios, for whom the universe is a single living whole in which every part is related to every other part in such a way that it can indicate the state of the other part and of the whole. In this way one can speak of a "cosmic symptomology": everything is a symptom of the state of everything else.

This is also the key to astrological belief, and its tremendous influence on the history of medicine. We never shall understand astrology, if we use for its interpretation the category of causality instead of that of analogy, and if we forget the presupposition of a cosmic sympathy. The qualities of the stars are represented in special ways in the different things and their qualities on earth. To know these qualities, to get them in pure form out of their surroundings is another phase of the magician's art. Alchemy is an offspring of this side of the magic world-view. And here again we must avoid the categories of our chemical thinking, especially that of substance. The hidden qualities of things are their special powers in the whole of sympathetic interrelations. Alchemy tries to discover not only these special powers, but also the highest, most valuable power, and to use it for the transformation of qualities, and, of course, for healing and other exercise of magical influence.

A Christian Neoplatonic bishop, Synesios, says: "Things besides being signs *of* each other have magic power *over* each other." He says this in his book on dreams, in which he praises the help he himself has received from them, and uses them as a proof of the power of divination. But here again we must not use our concept of ego. The universal sympathetic interdependence, that we find supposed everywhere from the most primitive tribes to the most refined of the Stoics and Neoplatonists, becomes unintelligible if we imagine that the sympathetic relation between beings is a relation between "egos" in the sense of individuals centered in their own consciousness. *Sympathein* (i.e., *pathein*, receiving influences, and *sym*, in direct contact and not through physical mediation) means a psychic participation in the other being, in knowing and acting. "Psychic" is here used, as it always should be, (1) *not* in the sense of occultistic, and (2) *not* in the sense of consciousness, but (3) as designating the sphere between the biological and the mental, as representing a middle sphere in which both these participate. This middle sphere can no longer be called "soul," since the Augustinian-Franciscan-Cartesian separation of soul and body has led to an identification of soul

26

and mind. The idea of a psychic participation of beings in each other by sympathetic contact excludes the application, not only of the notions of causality, substance, and ego in their ordinary sense, but also of the category of identity. For the concept of sympathetic contact breaks through the categorical idea of the exclusiveness of things and persons. The concept of "mystical participation," which Levy-Bruhl, in describing primitive mentality, calls one of non-Aristotelian logic, is rather one of a non-Aristotelian ontology, namely a magic one. This is especially important for the understanding of "spirits" in magic. He who exercises magical power is able to impose his will on spirits, and especially upon unclean or evil spirits. Spirits are not egos, nor are they things in terms of physical reality. They are forces of psychic character. *Pneumata*, *Geister*, *Ghosts*, are terms pointing to a nature which is neither mental nor physical, neither universal nor individual. "Breath," the root from which these words are derived, refers to the life-spirit, a sphere between the biological and the mental.

It is worth while to note that not even Descartes could complete his doctrine of man without calling in the mediating power of the vital spirit. Furthermore, it is wrong to call spirits living beings, thereby using the categoy of thing, a derivate from substance. The spirits are psychic forces *in* things, but not things themselves. This point leads to a further critical observation about the categorial structure of magic-sympathetic thinking, which is important in view of the reproof of superstition raised against it. The magical world-view appears superstitious if interpreted in terms of the category of "thing," or in terms of the categories which constitute the objective world of scientific analysis and rational technique. The idea of spirits as things or persons is a superstition. But spirits as psychic forces are a reality, or, at least, a potentiality. The transformation of a psychic force into a being with the character of a thing or person may be considered a "projection." And superstition in magic, as well as in religion, is the establishment of projections as objects. But if this be prevented, then elements of the magic-sympathetic world-view can be taken seriously again, for as Jung says: "Instead of being exposed to wild beasts, man is exposed today to the elemental forces of his own psyche. Psychic life is a world-power, that exceeds by many times all the powers of the earth."[16]

It seems to me most important for the whole problem of religion and health to recognize that the magical world-view is not religion, no more nor less so than is the physical world-view. It was in the name of religion, as well as of science, that Robert Boyle fought against the Hippocratean "physics" and the Paracelsian "archaeus" as idols set up between God and the world. The word "nature," which before Leibnitz and Kant had magical connotations, should be replaced, he said, by the word "mechanism" coined by Boyle himself. God made the world as a mechanism of great perfection but without a power of its own. This synthesis of a Calvinistic and a Cartesian attitude toward nature shows that religion can accept a scientific world-view as well as a magical one. Religion is not magic and magic is not religion. *Religion is the relation to something ultimate, unconditioned, transcendent.* The religious attitude is consciousness of *dependence* (cf. Schleiermacher's unconditional dependence), *surrender* (cf. Eckhard's *Entwerdung*, mystical annihilation, or Calvin's absolute obedience), *acceptance* (cf. Luther's taking, not giving, as first in religion). It concerns the whole man, is person-centered and ethical.

Stated in this way, the distinction between religion and magic is a clear and simple one. Magic is a special kind of interrelation between finite powers; religion is the human relation to infinite power and value. Magic can be creative and destructive, while religion stands essentially against destructive powers. Magic is the exercise of immanent power, religion is the subjection to the transcendent power, etc. But these differences are clearly visible only on the basis of a religious development in which prophetic or mystical criticism has definitely established the unconditional character of the Unconditioned, or the ultimate character of the Ultimate. And even then, the distinction is permanently endangered from two sides. First, there is the necessity that the transcendent manifests itself concretely, and, thereupon, these concrete manifestations become for the religious imagination magic powers. And secondly, there is the natural desire of man to gain power over the divine, thus making it an object of magical practices.

The divine beings or gods are the most important example of

28

the first danger. They are bearers of the Ultimate in being and in what ought to be, the two sides of every religion. But they are, at the same time, "powers," whose plurality indicates that none of them is really ultimate. Thus, they represent religious meaning, but in magic terms. The prophetic, as well as the mystical, battle against so-called polytheism was the world-historical way of liberating religion from identification with magic. But this battle can never come to an end, for the necessary ambiguity of every image of the divine is a permanent problem of religion, philosophy, and theory of man. On the subjective side, if dreams and visions of a typically psychic character play the role of means of religious revelation, then the spiritual is experienced in the form of the psychic. Hence, religion must pay continuous attention to the criteria of revelatory experiences. If they belong only to the universe of sympathy, which is the psychic universe, they can not be considered revelations in the religious sense. But if, in spite of having the general structure of magical sympathy, they are the bearers of *an ultimate, unconditioned concern*, then they are religious. Spiritualistic movements and their assumed revelations keep the necessity of a criterion very urgently before both theology and psychology.

Examples of the second danger to a true concept of religion, arising from the human attempt to gain a magical influence over the divine powers, are abundant. The magical distortion of prayer, from a form of union with the Ultimate symbolized as divine will or divine ground, into a form of using higher powers for personal purposes, is not only one of the most obvious phenomena in the history of religion, but it is a continuous temptation in every high religion, and every Christian minister can witness to it. The form of prayer necessarily has this ambiguity, which can not lead religion, however, to the dropping of this form, as some radical Protestant theologians are inclined to do, but only to a continuous attention to the danger of confusing the magical and the religious. Equally refined is the amalgamation of these two in the sacramental sphere. The Reformers attacked the magical distortion of the sacraments in the Roman church. For them the idea that the sacraments have an effect beyond the conscious center of the personality through their mere performance (*opus operatum*) was magic. Instead of it, they demanded the "word" which appeals to consciousness and evokes man's answer in a personal decision. Thereby they left to Protestant theology the practically unsolved problem of the meaning of the sacraments.

The examples show that, while the distinction between religion and magic is logically ambiguous, in reality there is always a certain ambiguity to be overcome. But the last example can help us to make still another step. The tension between a religion of the word and a religion of the sacrament indicates a polarity in the nature of religion itself. Indeed, exclusive emphasis on the person-centered pole in Protestantism and some types of Judaism, found opposition, not only from the Catholic and semi-Catholic side, but also from within these groups themselves. Schleiermacher's definition of religion as a kind of feeling, rightly interpreted by Rudolf Otto as "numinous" experience, was one inroad from the other pole within Protestantism. Others are seen in movements for liturgical reform and for religious healing. It appears very significant that, according to Professor Murray of Harvard, "the tendency to form complexes is on the average most frequent in Jews, Protestants occupying the second place, and Catholics only the third."

A widespread interpretation of magic holds it to be true in principle in so far as it is based on "suggestion," perhaps including telepathy. This assumption has weight because it would explain a great deal of the effectiveness of magical practices, especially in the realm of healing. It is important to note that this explanation involves re-establishing a sphere in which man is neither mind nor body in the Cartesian sense, but something intermediate. "To suggest" (i.e., to bring under the skin, sc., into the unconscious) has a double meaning. On the one hand, it designates a hint, an insinuation, a proposal whereby the freedom of him who receives the suggestion is preserved. On the other hand, it designates the introduction or stimulation of an idea of impulse in somebody whereby his freedom is disregarded. The second concept is the important one for our problem, but in many, perhaps in most cases, there is no sharp boundary line between the two meanings. A suggested idea is accepted with the help of the suggestive power of somebody. The role of suggestion in the cause and treatment of disease among primitives and among ourselves is not very different, thinks Rivers.[17] Hypnotism is an extreme case of suggestion, and, according to Rivers, even if this extreme form is not used, the action of suggestion in any form of medical treatment can never be excluded. According to Myers, suggestion can be defined as "the process of effectively impressing upon the subliminal intelligence the wishes of a man's own supraliminal self or that of some other person."[18] The concept of "magnetism," used by Paracelsus and Mesmer, points to the same thing that Maxwell recommended as sympathetic cure by external and internal suggestion. From the temple incubation at the Asclepian center in Kos to the miraculous cures of Our Lady of Lourdes, suggestion, through dreams, visions, and religious faith, has played an important part. Dawson sums up his ideas in this statement: "The entire outlook on life may be altered by the practice of religious suggestions, especially autosuggestions."[19]

But, beyond both of these forms of suggestion, the highest healing power is that of faith, because this involves the spiritual center of man. The ambiguity of the whole situation is thus indicated, for the magical and the religious spheres are again seen to merge in what is called "religious suggestion." Yet Hiltner is right in stressing that genuine religious healing is not by suggestions. We must ask, however, is it without suggestion? I myself do not believe that this is ever possible. For, besides the conscious acceptance of an idea or a demand, elements of the situation always sink into the unconscious and have effects. The suggestive power of a Catholic mass in a medieval cathedral, or of a revivalist in a denominational camp-meeting, or of a minister alongside a sickbed are realities which can not be denied or removed by religious purism. But the question must be raised whether the elements which grasp the unconscious are bearers of the Ultimate, and whether they are received by the total personality instead of remaining strange bodies within it.

By holding on to this question a decision can be given concerning the relation of healing by suggestion and healing by faith. But, first, it is necessary to liberate the word "faith" from all inferior connotations (e.g., as opinion without much evidence, or acceptance of authorities on irrational grounds, or subjection to foreign or auto-suggestion), and to restore it to its true religious sense, in which faith is the state of being grasped by the Ultimate. Then we can say that healing in the spiritual or genuine religious sense is

31

mediated by faith. And this act of being made whole in relation to the ultimate ground and meaning of our existence influences all sides of our personality in the direction of wholeness, psyche, mind, and body. But the term "faith-healing" becomes inappropriate for such an event. For it is ordinarily used for cases of an evidently suggestive character, and healing with religious material through suggestion is not religious healing in the sense just indicated. In every case it is necessary to ask how faith and suggestion are related to each other. The suggested material may appear in an act of genuine faith, or it may not. And, likewise, healing through auto-suggestion with religious ideas may be an occasion for faith, or, again, a factor working against real faith.

A note on ecstasy.
The ancient physicians and medical philosophers took a keen interest in excessive emotions and their ambiguous character. Emotionally violent love was considered a kind of mental disease wherein the boundary between creative and destructive alienation became dubious. Plato says that where the action of the soul is too strong, it attracts the body so powerfully that it throws it into a consuming state, and either divine mania or mental illness is the result. Aristotle believed that mental illness often adds to the creative functioning of a personality. Similarly, in the New Testament some of the demoniacs recognize Jesus as the Christ better than do normal people. In early Christianity the mentally ill were, for a certain time, cherished as holy. Charcot called ecstatic individuals among the mentally disturbed the "aristocrats of the possessed." In the debates between the somatologists and the psychologists (or between the "brain-mythologists" and the "theologians," as they called each other!) the problem of the boundary line between creative and destructive "insanity" played a great role. "The genius may be insane and yet be a genius, a valuable, if not at times the most valuable, asset to civilization,"[20] says Zilboorg. He rightly points to the many mentally ill geniuses at the end of the nineteenth century. Reil goes even farther, and demands a kind of mental illness of every man as the starting-point of an intellectual life.

There was and still is a fear today that psychoanalysis may make a man normal and insignificant. The problem is very important from the point of view of the relation between religion and health, because experience of the Ultimate essentially and necessarily has some ecstatic character. Thus the question arises in what way is religion healthy and in what way not, and again what is the relation between creative and destructive ecstasy. The question has a bearing upon the theory of depth-psychology itself. For if the interpretation of insanity as the breaking of the unconscious into consciousness is right, and genius and religious ecstasy are also interpreted similarly, then there must be assumed either two aspects of the unconscious, or two ways of the invasion of consciousness by the unconscious: a creative, divine one, and a destructive, demonic one. Judged by a spiritual standard, in either case the unconscious as such, or its way of acting, its darkness and primitivity, exhibits a dubious character.

Concepts of nature and their implications.
In connection with Boyle's attack on Paracelsus and Hippocrates we have already pointed to the ambiguity of the concept of "nature." It involves more than two millenniums of battle between the Pythagorean-Platonic and the Aristotelean-Hippocratean understanding of nature. The very fact that neither could prevail decisively against the other, and that today the theory of *Gestalt* and the rediscovery of the psychic realm has deprived the quantitative-mechanistic definition of nature of its seemingly uncontested victory, shows that nature has two faces, the one turned toward matter, the other toward the soul. Plotinus' metaphysical symbolism is right when he says that the bodily world is posited between *psyche* and *hyle*. Descartes removed the psychic sphere by calling the soul the conscious ego and denying to it the face turned to the psyche, and, by calling nature a mechanism and denying to it the face which it also turns psyche-ward. We have already seen that both concepts of nature, the mechanical and the vital, are compatible with religion. But there is a strong affinity, on the one hand, between the "religion of the word" and the Cartesian concept of nature, and on the other, between the Paracelsian nature concept and the "religion of the sacrament." And in Cartesian terms it is difficult to make of religious healing more than an inexplicable act of divine providence.

33

A note on psychotherapy and freedom.
A further reason for the cutting off of medicine from the psyche was the protest of jurists against a medical interpretation of mental disturbances. They wanted to maintain the responsibility of witches and sorcerers for their acts, and freedom of decision seemed to be endangered by medical interpretations. So the famous Bodin, in his defense of demonology against the enlightened attacks of Johann Weyer, who said "the witches are mentally sick people," prophesied the breakdown of penal jurisprudence and of general morals, if medical determinism were applied to the explanation of mental disorder. Today the same discussion is going on between psychotherapists and religious or secular representatives of moral and social conformism. Psychological explanations seem to destroy responsibility. Psychic mechanisms, compulsions, and their methodological healing seem to deny personal freedom. To this Zilboorg answers that the psychic apparatus is not the soul in the spiritual sense, but an "organ," and that deficiencies or malfunctions of this psychic organ vitiate the free exercise of the will as much as do those of the brain. This is not altogether convincing, because the psychic drives have not the same relation to the conscious center of personality as the brain has to the psychological functions. Yet Zilboorg is seeking for the solution in a right direction. The question which must be asked, and which will be asked in the context of our last section, is this: In how far is the conscious center of the personality the resultant of unconscious factors, individual and collective, and in how far are these factors directed towards the unity of the personal center? The same question has been raised above in connection with the problem of creative ecstasy. On the answer to this problem depends the practical attitude of the healer toward the amount of freedom he can presuppose and use in working for a new balance in the patient, and the further evaluation of moral and religious means as influencing neurotics.

Divergent historical trends leading to a basic question

In the history of religion and healing there are certain trends which are important for the understanding of our present situation. There is a trend, which appears in religion as well as in healing, toward an idea and ideal of purity, and there is a different trend in both toward another idea and ideal of harmony. Each of these will be briefly discussed. And then the conflict of these divergent trends will be discussed as leading to the central problem of their theory of man, namely, whether he is a dynamic unity or a static composite.

The trend toward the idea of purity.
The demand for purity is effective on different levels. In biblical accounts one can distinguish the physical cleanness of the body; an antiseptic cleanness of sanitation; medical cleanness (as when certified by the priest in cases of leprosy); psychic cleanness (after the exorcism of demonic possession); ritual cleanness (such as menstrual taboos, etc.); dietary cleanness (in which sanitary and ritual elements are united); cleanness of heart (that is, of the whole personality, which is the condition for the indwelling of the divine spirit and the vision of God); moral cleanness (especially related to the sexual realm); sacramental cleanness (such as baptism and other rites of purification in which moral and ritual elements are united); the cleanness of holiness (which is divine, and can be recovered by man only through divine forgiveness, and the purging of impure elements from the soul and the community).

But in all these cases, the simple physical image of a foreign body intruding into the realm of the "whole," is presupposed: filth, infection, contagion, demonic influences, black magic, forbidden food, sexual or idolatrous pollution, and finally, "sin" as an objective, half-demonic reality. On the basis of this symbolism, healing and salvation take on the character of purification. All the various levels on which the idea of cleanness appears can be found in the Persian-Jewish-Christian development. (The "dirty monk" who, for ascetic reasons, boasts of his bodily uncleanliness, and whose soul often reveals the same uncleanness, is not genuinely Christian, but the result of an invasion of Oriental asceticism, for which the body as such is unclean. It is in fundamental contradiction to the teaching of the Old Testament.) But the different levels may become independent, and when they do, distortions of the idea of cleanness occur, some of them fateful.

35

Thus modern Protestantism, especially of the Anglo-Saxon type, created a cult of physical cleanness, with extreme emphasis on moral purity, but largely unaware of the infected soul with its "unclean spirits." In Lutheranism, the exclusive emphasis on the clean conscience through the forgiveness of sins, overlooks uncleanness in the moral and psychic realms. Modern medicine brought antiseptic cleanness to perfection, but it was not interested in psychological purification, or cleanness of the "heart." The Church stressed ritual and sacramental purification more and more, to the increasing neglect of cleanness of heart and of holiness. Most dangerous was the fear of unclean spirits and their magic which produced the witchcraft delusion of the Middle Ages, and resulted in persecution of the mentally ill (the bearers of non-ecclesiastical magic power), as well as of heretics. Since this kind of possession involves the whole personality (including the body) except the "immortal soul," which could still be saved, burning was the logical method of eliminating demonic uncleanness from the victim, and from society.

This short survey of the idea of purity in religion and healing has shown that religious symbolism is not an accidental imagery which could be replaced by other images, but is rooted in a real unity of the realm from which the symbols are taken (the bodily sphere) with the realm in which they function (the mental sphere). The well-known neurotic type of compulsive cleanliness and the corresponding psychological type are not just types of individuals, but are, also, potential bearers of objective values, and potential forces of destruction of values. Although the relation between the different levels of cleanness is by no means that of simple interdependence, still less is it that of simple indifference. Healing and salvation, as well, are "states of uncleanness."

The trend toward harmony in religion and healing.
The implication of "uncleanness" is that a disturbing factor has penetrated into the "whole" from outside, but equally plausible, and even more important, is the idea of disturbances in the "whole" itself. This presupposes that the "whole" is a harmony of contrasting forces. This idea was first expressed in connection with health, bodily and psychic, by the Pythagorean Alkmaion, in his concept of "isonomy." Later it became the basis of the

36

great development of Greek medicine in Hippocrates and Galen, who considered disease as a disturbance of the harmonious constitution of the body based on the balance of *dynameis*, or juices. The task of medicine was to discover the types of deviation from the normal, harmonious structure, which is analogous to the harmony in music, sculpture, and personal ethos. This led to the identification of health and beauty, and to the oft abused formula, *Mens sana in corpore sano*. In spite of his hostility toward the academically fixed and traditionally authoritative medicine of Galen, Paracelsus accepts the idea of "dynamic harmony" in his medical-religious world view. Gundolf says, "As a theologian and as a physician, he deals not with concepts or things but with forces."[21] "He did not seek for substances like the ancients, nor for laws like the moderns, but for forces"; He was equally removed from the "magic concepts" still powerful in his period, and from the mechanical causality which grew powerful after him."[22] But he saw the harmony of the body within the frame of the larger harmony of the cosmos, for the "Macrocosmos is often ill like the microcosmos." The physician must, therefore, know all the forces of life, in stones and metals, in plants and animals, in man individual and social, up to God and Satan.

We find this dynamic harmonism again in romantic medicine (and theology), especially in the romantic psychotherapists, Gross, Ideler, and Feuchtersleben, of whom Zilboorg says, "These generations [1800-1850] spoke the very language which the majority of the medical psychologists of the fifth decade of the twentieth century speak."[23] They knew about "drives of freedom," "strivings to infinity," "diseases of personality," etc. Schelling, the leading philosopher of this period, tried to describe the struggling forces in terms which have at the same time an ontological, biological, and psychological character, following and rationalizing Paracelsus and Boehme, and uniting again the natural, the psychic, and the religious.

The present day dynamic psychology of the unconscious belongs clearly to this line of thought, from which it borrows much conceptual material, especially the basic idea of illness as the disturbance of a dynamic balance by conflicting drives, which it has confirmed empirically. Zilboorg sounds like a psychologized Schelling when he says, "When unconscious psychological reality dominates the real world ... mental disease occurs."[24] He praises Freud as the discoverer of the *dynamic* power of the unconscious, and says, "The drives are nothing but a mass of undifferentiated impulses which make man move on and live ..."[25] He expresses the principle of dynamic balance clearly by pointing to the threat to reason "when the psychic apparatus is disturbed in the quantitative relationship of its parts,"[26] or by saying, "the strength of the ego is not to be measured by the keenness of our sensory-motor system, but rather by the ability of the ego to balance and to integrate the drives of the id and the claims of the super-ego."[27] He stresses the point that it is the *integration* of the drives, and not the abolishment of any of them, that brings about health. In Jung's system, the lack of balance between the unconscious and the conscious (or between the "id" and the "ego," to use Freudian terms) is enlarged to cosmic dimensions. This, too, is in the Paracelsus-Schelling line, through Jung himself is careful to avoid ontological statements. But it is difficult to deny ontological implications in his statements concerning the ritual and the dogmatic conceptions of primitive religions, and of Christianity, that "they were dams and walls erected against the dangers of the unconscious, the 'perils of the soul.'"[28] And, in a statement similar to Zilboorg's, he says, "the unconscious is capable of taking over the rôle of the ego. The result of this exchange is chaos and destruction ..."[29]

Paracelsus was interested in the diseases of special social groups; so, too, the latest supporters of the principle of dynamic balance, especially in psychiatry, have seen this problem, and have emphasized the interdependence of the individual and the social element in disease and healing. Zilboorg says, "Mental diseases are apparently the only diseases which deserve the appellation of social diseases.... A psychological conflict leading to disease cannot but use as its vehicle the sum total of the cultural problems which are characteristic of the individual's age."[30] This phrasing is more cautious than that of Freud, who believed in neuroses and psychoses of a civilization, and considered religion as a mass neurosis. Zilboorg calls this "organic anthropomorphism" and says, "A community can no more suffer from a neurosis than it can suffer from pneumonia."[1] Nevertheless, he admits that "any society which would offer no outlets to our

38

repressed, forbidden drives would probably crumble under the very weight of the accumulated power of undischarged drives,"[32] and that "the culture of our day militates to a great extent against the truly genital integration of man's instinctual life."[33] Quotations in a similar vein from Hiltner, Horney, and Fromm, could be multiplied at will, not to mention Jung's conception of the "collective unconscious."

In the religious sphere, the classical expression for wholeness is "the peace of God" which, according to St. Paul, exceeds all *nous* (rational understanding), and which is able to safeguard the heart (the center of personality) and the *noemata* (acts of rational understanding). The "peace of God" (or "peace of Christ") is the exact opposite of "man against himself." It is "man *reconciled*" and thereby re-established in his essential and created harmony. Without using the word peace, Hiltner sums up the function of religious healing in the following description: "Real spiritual healing brings forgiveness, . . . after the real guiltiness has been recognized, . . . reorganization, after the powerful elements of disorganization have been investigated, . . . love, after one's capacities for hostility have been seen, . . . security, after one's anxieties have been understood."[34] Similarly, in his defense of religion against Freud's "self-contradictory" attacks, Zilboorg says: "Both religion and psychoanalysis . . . seek the path that would lead to serenity; . . . both seem to have solved the problem on the basis of the same principle, . . . love."[35] He might have quoted Plato: "Harmonious love between the elements is the source of health; wanton love, the source of disease."

If we compare the idea of harmony with the idea of purity in its function for religion and medicine, we find that the trend toward divergence of the various realms in which cleanness is demanded has no analogy in the functioning of the idea of harmony. On the contrary, wherever the latter idea is predominant, religious and medical healing are convergent. So it is today; so it was in the age of Romanticism, in the Renaissance, and in Pythagoreanism. The reason for this is obvious: bodily infection is understandable without reference to the personality as a whole, but the inner disturbance of a given harmony drives beyond any peripheral causation to the central cause, the personality itself. But neither of these historical ideas proved decisive for the union or separation of religion and healing. What was and is decisive is the question of whether man must be considered as a dynamic unity of diverse elements, or as a static composite of different parts. If the first alternative be accepted, religion, psychiatry, and medicine are united, though not identified; if the second be accepted, religion and medicine are separated, and psychiatry is swallowed up by one or the other.

Is man a dynamic unit or a static composite?
A few of Stefan Zweig's sweeping statements may serve to pose the question:

The physician puts himself beside the priest, and very soon against him. . . . Disease is no longer something which concerns the whole man, but something which hits one of his organs. . . . The laboratory keeps the doctor from a practical insight into the personality of the patient; the hospital keeps him from a personal contact with the patient. The family doctor, who knew the human being as the sick person, and in whom a kind of union of priest and healer had survived, is speedily disappearing. . . . The expert in every section of body and soul replaces him. But the more technical, scientific, and departmentalized medicine becomes, the more the people react against it. They mind it that the healer has become a scientist, they feel instinctively that disease is not localized but concerns the whole constitution, the body as well as psyche and spirit.[36]

It is along the same line when Sigerist shows how different classical Greek medicine was from ours. It was "constitutional" and not "organic" medicine. Hippocrates' *Prognosticon* introduces total diagnosis, instead of inspection of the urine. For the Greeks, healing was basically an *art*, and, as Sigerist says, "The medical art is much less dependent on the medical science than is usually supposed. The art is the eternal in medicine."[37] Today "science is in the process of strangling the medical art."[38] But even more, healing is not dependent on the physician (only a small proportion of the sick go to a physician); there is self-healing, medical folk-lore, and religious healing, all of which trespass upon the domain of medical science and art. Significant was the

40

lack of anatomy in Greece, which prevented the treatment of "sick organs" instead of sick people, and created a strong emphasis on dietetics and hygiene of body and soul.

In contradistinction to the lack of anatomy in Greek medicine, modern medicine is completely tied to anatomy. Sigerist remarks that the Occident found its proper medical expression in the anatomic principle.[39] It is significant that Vesalius calls his classical book on anatomy *De corporis humani fabrica*. Surgery is the practical consequence, and its triumphant successes the confirmation of this ideal. Using the knife is correcting anatomically. All attempts to withdraw from the anatomical ideal were without success. Even a physiologist like William Harvey, discoverer of the circulation of the blood, created only a dynamic anatomy, an *anatomia animata*, in the baroque style.[40] The victory of the anatomic ideal was decided by Descartes, with his elimination of the realm of the psychic for the sake of pure consciousness on the one hand, and pure extension on the other. The body, belonging to the realm of extension, became a machine of which the parts could be amended without affecting the whole. The mind, on the other hand, was the object of a psychology of consciousness, while the whole realm between was eliminated by an act of extreme philosophical radicalism.[41] Philosophers of this school "divided man sharply into a body and a soul, . . . they were purely materialistic when they looked at the body, and as purely idealistic when they contemplated the soul."[42] "An intermediate area between the body and the soul and yet within the perishable frame of man seemed to them unthinkable."[43]

This indicates that the basic problem in the relation of religion and health is the "intermediate area," the psychic, including the unconscious, the "drives," — that which is open to magic or psychotherapy. The whole doctrine of man is centered in this problem, and so is medical anthropology. It is especially the understanding of mental illness which demands an understanding of the middle area, and of the totality of the human personality. Mental illness has been considered either as a symptom of bodily illness, or of religious and moral depravity. In the first case, it was in the hands of the physicians; in the second, in the hands of priests, educators, and judges. The two solutions exhausted the possibilities: since the "soul" was not distinguished from the psy-

41

che, it could not become ill; if there was illness, it was bodily; if not, mental derangement must be regarded as the fall of the immortal soul. In no case could a *mental* illness be imagined.

But the situation was not really as simple as that. In spite of the moral character of mental illness (still effective in the popular attitude toward psychotics and neurotics), it is different from other forms of immorality: it has the character of "possession." This does not make it less but *more* punishable, but the method of dealing with it is different. The healing of possession has magic-exorcistic character, and is neither merely natural nor merely moral. Awareness of the middle sphere thus existed and was often expressed, but a method of dealing with it directly and independently of body and spirit was lacking. "Psychiatry, almost from the moment it was delivered from the womb of medicine in the days of Hippocrates, was kidnapped and brought up in the strange home of theology and in the flowery, multi-colored gardens of abstract philosophy."[44] But, in spite of its captivity, it survived and left its traces in the history of religion and medicine, for the reality on which it is based cannot be destroyed: that middle area, which decides for man's unity against his division, and which, therefore, is also the condition of the unity of religion and medicine. Hippocrates recognized the physical cause of epilepsy, the traditionally "sacred disease," and is often regarded as the father of a medicine which separated itself not only from psychiatry but also from religion. But, on the contrary, he knew about the influence of the passions, and their affects on the production of disease, and this knowledge was not lost for a long time.

We find a continuing awareness of the special character of mental disease in Cicero (*Tusculana* III), for instance: "Why is it that this art has so badly neglected the ... healing of the soul ... what bodily diseases can be more serious than those two diseases of distress and desire?" He even protests against the word, melancholy, because it is not purely psychological. There were excellent observations concerning the dynamics of drives and mental disease as affecting the whole personality in such writers as Plutarch, Celsus, and Aretaeus, but the revival of oriental demonology in the noble form of Neoplatonism was too strong. Caelius speaks already of a special type of demon who seduces women.[45]

"Psychiatry finally became a study of the ways and means of the devil and his cohorts." The magic realm was occupied by religion, and exorcism became a main way of healing. "The clergy excluded psychiatry from medicine but was unable to abolish it. It merely reappeared under the name of demonology."[46] This is confirmed by the fact that Charcot, in his description of "major hysteria," could include the *stigmata diaboli* from medieval books on demonology.

In order to understand this merger of religion and psychiatry, we must keep in mind that the magic powers in the Neoplatonic system, though not the Ultimate, are degrees leading to it. They are semi-divine, and that means, from a monotheistic point of view, demonic beings usurping divine quality. This is the reason why demonic possession and heresy (service of a demonic deity) could be identified, and both found in some cases of mental illness. The battle against mental disease had become an inner religious battle; the psychic and the spiritual were united, but both were separated from medicine. If the physician could not find a physical cause for mental disturbances, the patient was turned over to the clergy. We can, therefore, say that it was a Christianized Neoplatonism which, by capturing the middle sphere of man, the psychic, first produced the gap between religion and healing. Religious (as well as legal and moral) opposition prevented the rise of psychiatry, even in the seventeenth century. In fact, at this time, philosophy became another factor working in the same direction. Following the Cartesian dichotomy, Kant demanded "that all the insane be turned over to the philosophers and that the medical men stop mixing into the business of the human mind."[47] This is, perhaps, the clearest expression of the loss of the middle sphere — as well as the most absurd! The reply of medicine, of course, could only be to take over the insane completely as people organically sick.

Against both extremes, however, the principle of unity through a middle sphere was maintained and supported by a good deal of empirical evidence. Stahl (about 1770), repelled by the increasing cleavage between body and mind, fought together with Cabanis for the wholeness of man. He discovered the source of mental disease in ideas contrary to the direction of the life force (called repression today). He found the difference between

43

organic and functional mental diseases, and, with it, an independent realm for psychiatry (a term rejected by the somatologists). From another side came an emphasis on suggestion and autosuggestion as the source of many human reactions, normal and abnormal (Bernheim and the school of Nancy). Here was the connecting link between ancient magic and the most advanced modern view. It would be interesting to show how, in the beginning of the twentieth century, a general attack was made on Cartesian dualism, and largely succeeded. Every realm of knowledge which deals with man as man participated, but in no realm were the weapons used against the idea of man as a static composite as strong and as deadly as those of medical psychology. Since Freud's description of the role of the unconscious in mental diseases and neuroses, the rediscovery of the intermediate sphere has proceeded with irresistible power.

The generally acknowledged term designating the unity of man's being is "personality," and a neurosis is a disturbance of the development of personality. Jung writes: "Behind the neurotic perversion is concealed vocation, destiny, the development of personality."[49] Personality develops in an individual as "a unique, indivisible unit, or 'whole man'."[49] The purpose of all healing is the "integration of personality." Personality means wholeness, a vocation performed. Hiltner, in a discussion of psychiatric terminology, decides in favor of "personality illness," or "personality disorder."[50] This includes a demand that physicians and psychiatrists take an interest in "positive health" as well as in "absence of illness,"[51] as is now the case: "A healthy interpretation of religion must be related to the whole personality."[52] Zilboorg expresses the principle of unity thus: "Modern dynamic psychology considers man in his totality and tries not to overlook the spirit in the animal that he is, or the animal in the spirit that he has,"[53] and, "any perpetuation of the old dichotomy of body and mind in medical science must militate against a proper scientific synthesis of psychological problems."[54] The principle of unity has conquered the principle of division, but now we must ask: What is the structure of this unity, and what are its consequences for the relation of religion and health?

44

The basic problem

In the course of this discussion, a certain number of problems have shown themselves, and for some of them solutions have been suggested. But the basic question still remains: What is the structural relation of the "middle sphere" of human nature, the "psychic" reality, to the spiritual and bodily realities? If this is answered (provisionally, of course, as in any scientific answer), the relations of the various ways of healing to each other can be derived from it.

It may be helpful here to make use of a model already referred to, which shows the mutual relations of the bodily, psychic, and mental spheres. This model, of which some elements were first conceived by Plotinus, in our context has no more significance than a model in physics or chemistry; it merely simplifies for descriptive purposes things which in reality are infinitely more complex.

It may be said in a mythical symbol, that, psyche turns one face toward mind and another toward body, and that, in the same way, body turns one face toward psyche and another toward *physis*, while the mind turns one face toward psyche and another toward reason. This indicates that in body, as well as in mind, there is something intimately united with the psychic sphere, and something alien to it and only indirectly united with it. The former assertion is an acceptance of the belief that man is a dynamic unity, while the latter makes it clear how the understanding of man as a static composite could have been developed successfully.

First, however, we must ask the question: What, in the light of our model, is the nature of the bodily or the biological sphere — life in the sense of living beings? Is the life process merely a complex physico-chemical mechanism whose perfection and duration can be enhanced by physical and chemical repairs? Or are the physical and chemical structures used by a "plan," an "entelechy," a "life principle" (which, of course, is not a causality along with others, but the direction in which the causes are effective)? In the first case, bodily medicine alone would suffice; neither from the psychic nor from the mental side could healing influences be expected. In the second case, influencing and

45

strengthening the living organism as a whole would direct the course of physico-chemical causality, and might produce healing effects. The age-old idea of the *vis medicatrix naturae* is in agreement with this presupposition. But the question is, what is this totality of causal chains which is "centered" or "directed" without the aid of an additional causality? The "ontological compulsion" always to apply the causal scheme, even where we must prohibit its use, may prevent us from ever gaining an insight into the nature of a life-centered causality. But, however we describe this structure, the center is not omnipotent, and the body is turned with one face toward *physis*, the physico-chemical realm, open to its influences, in disorder, disintegration, and healing. This is the justification for the relative independence of purely medical methods and the "anatomic pattern" despite criticism from all kinds of "natural healing."

The second question refers to the relationship of the psychic element to the rational element in the nature of the mind. Reason, in the classical sense, is the system of categories, structures, and universals, which have practical and theoretical validity (however the ontological nature of this validity and the possibility of knowing it, is thought of). In each of its acts the mind is related to the reasonable structure of reality, but in such a way that it drives beyond any special element, and even beyond the universe itself, toward the ultimate ground and meaning of the whole and the special forms within it. This "driving beyond" in asking and receiving is what we mean by religion.

The mind is directed towards the valid norms and structures of reality (the Scholastics called this *intentionalitas*, directedness towards the objectively valid) as the mathematician's mind is directed toward valid equations. But the mind is also directed toward the *bearer* of intentionality, the psyche with its striving forces, for without these psychic forces no mental act is possible. But even more, the contents of the mental acts are determined, not only by the objective structures of reality, but also by the psychic reception of them. How is this possible? It would be impossible if the mind were something like a logical machine — corresponding to the physical machine of the physico-chemical interpretation of life — guided by clear and distinct insights, and misguided by the lack of perfect perceptions. In this case, the psychic sphere could only be regarded as a disturbing element in the operation of the mind. Mental and spiritual healing would be unthinkable. In so far as the mind is concerned, no healing would be needed, only enlightenment (cf. Kant's demand that the mentally ill be turned over to the philosophers), and, in so far as illness is concerned, it would be purely bodily.

The opposite solution regards the contents of the mind as "sublimations" of psychic drives. But the term sublimation is ambiguous; it can deny the objective validity of the results of the sublimation, in which case the "principle of reality" is abandoned, and all the contents of religion and culture are *nothing but* projections of psychic instincts. This is absurd, because it undermines the theory of sublimation as much as any other theory. Or, sublimation may be regarded as the process in which the unconscious drives are united with valid contents, in which case it states the problem of the relation of psyche and mind, but does not solve it. Is there any way of formulating the psychic-mental unity? "Man uses his animal instincts in order to build his loftiest ideals and . . . his loftiest ideals consequently derive their energies from his animal drives, albeit domesticated."[55] This would seem to imply that the instincts are, though in a primitive or undomesticated form, essentially related to the contents of the mind, i.e., to religion and culture. Furthermore, it seems to imply that the rational side of mental questioning derives its creative and dynamic power from a prerational element in the mind, which may be called feeling, affect, passion, emotion (the terminology is very unstable). This prerational element would direct the rational element in a specific direction; thus, religion and culture would be based on a *union of structure and passion*. If this formulation is acceptable (though probably no more understandable than life-centered causality), it would be more than mere poetry to say, in the spirit of St. Augustine, that the drives originating in the psyche are restless until they find rest in union with the mind. And mental healing would be the art of helping this union come to pass by guiding the psychic forces in that direction in which, by their very nature, they want to go in order to find rest.

There is something in the structure of mind and reality which transcends itself, not toward another, higher realm, but toward a special qualification of both the prerational and rational ele-

47

ments, i.e., the spiritual. The spiritual is not a sphere outside the mind, as the Unconditioned is not a reality outside the conditioned, nor the Ultimate a stage above the preliminary. The spiritual is a qualification of the mind, the Unconditioned is a dimension of the conditioned, and the Ultimate is the point of reference for everything preliminary. All creations of the mind have such a spiritual element, in so far as they have an ultimate meaning and significance. Therefore, any attempt to guide the psychic drives must take into consideration not only the mental contents as such, but also their hidden or manifest spiritual qualification.

Spiritual healing is the depth-dimension of mental healing; it is potentially, if not actually present, whether it expresses itself in the seriousness and profundity of the psycho-therapeutic situation, or in explicit religious manifestations. However, it is also true that mental healing — and through it bodily healing — is a potential, though not always actual, consequence of spiritual healing, whether an intentional one, as in religious couselling, or unintentionally produced by preaching and liturgy. These distinctions should prevent a confusion of functions: the spirituality of a psychiatric situation is not dependent on any religious reference; nor is the psychic power of a religious situation dependent on any psychiatric reference.

And now we must introduce a great simplification of our model. We must say that the face the psyche turns toward the body, and the face the body turns toward the psyche, constitute a common sphere; and that the face the psyche turns toward the mind, and the face the mind turns toward the psyche, also constitute a common sphere. The vital and the unconscious drives are the same, seen from two sides; and the prerational process of the mind and the conscious process of the psyche are the same, seen from two sides. The latter statement is corroborated by Zilboorg: "A psychological phenomenon is a biological function for which no specialized organ is found in the living organism."[56] "Fear, love, hatred, admiration, sense of guilt and remorse, sense of righteousness and indignation, compassion and contempt — every shade of human emotions"[57] are total functions, and, as such, are the concern of the psychiatrists.

There is, consequently, psychic reality in the body and in the mind; the first, unconscious, the second, conscious, and the ques-

48

tion which finally must be answered is: How are these two sides related to each other. The answer, derived from our model, must be: The unconscious becomes actually what it potentially is, and for which it strives, by reaching the state of consciousness; and the consciousness includes the potentialities driving within the unconscious as its vital reservoir. Potentiality is not actuality, but neither is it nothing; it is *potentia*, power: the most destructive power, if it conquers the mental unity of consciousness after having been repressed; the most creative power, if it enters and widens the consciousness through union with the integration (or disintegration) of the personality; it decides between disease and health, and between destruction and salvation.

In describing the model which is supposed to represent the dynamic unity of man, I have avoided the terms "ego," "self," "superego," and I have but seldom used the term "personality," for the reason that each of these terms has obvious ambiguities, and requires constant revision of its connotations. "Ego" has the epistemological connotation of the Cartesian *ego cogitans*, but the center of consciousness which mediates between reason and the unconscious is more than the subject of knowledge. "The self" is a less abused, though more artificial, term, and it expresses more fully the dymanic character of man's personal life. "Superego" sounds like another and higher ego, a magic power, created by social repression. It is a very unfortunate word, if it is supposed to express the objective and categorical character of the structure of reality over against the arbitrariness of the drives, for this structure is nothing like an ego, even if projected or symbolized as such. The term personality is a mixture of a normative and a descriptive term: if we say that someone is a "personality," in contrast to others who are not, the word is normative; if, however, we speak of "diseases of personality," the word is descriptive, for everyone is subject to them. The indefinite character of modern psychological terminology reveals the immature stage of the self-interpretation of man in our age.

The questions asked here in the form of suggested answers may serve as starting points for questions still remaining to be asked.

1. G.G. Dawson, *Healing: Pagan and Christian* (London, 1935), p. 124.
2. Seward Hiltner, *Religion and Health* (New York, 1943), p. 23.
3. Dawson, *op. cit.*, p. 57.

4. Hiltner, *op. cit.*, p. 100.

5. Quoted by Dawson, *op. cit.*, p. 150.

6. Friedrich Gundolf, *Paracelsus*, (Berlin, 1928), p. 50.

7. *Ibid.*, p. 71.

8. *Ibid.*, p. 589.

9. Dawson, *op. cit.*, p. viii.

10. Hiltner, *op. cit.*, p. 100.

11. Gregory Zilboorg, *A History of Medical Psychology* (New York, 1941), p. 33.

12. *Ibid.*, p. 155.

13. *Ibid.*, pp. 354 f.

14. Lynn Thorndike, *The Place of Magic in the Intellectual History of Europe* (New York, 1905), p. 34.

15. *Ibid.*, p. 29.

16. Carl G. Jung, *The Integration of the Personality* (New York, 1940), p. 293.

17. W.H.R. Rivers, *Medicine, Magic, and Religion* (London, 1924), p. 50.

18. Dawson, *op. cit.*, p. 294.

19. *Ibid.*, p. 304.

20. Zilboorg, *op. cit.*, p. 463.

21. Gundolf, *op. cit.*, p. 52.

22. *Ibid.*, p. 101.

23. Zilboorg, *op. cit.*, p. 48®.

24. *Ibid.*, p. 489.

25. Zilboorg, *Mind, Medicine and Man* (New York, 1943), p. 82.

26. *Ibid.*, p. 329.

27. *Ibid.*, p. 103.

28. Jung, *op. cit.*, p. 71.

29. *Ibid.*, p. 7.

30. Zilboorg, *A History of Medical Psychology*, p. 523.

31. Idem, *Mind, Medicine and Man*, p. 198.

32. *Ibid.*, p. 211.

33. *Ibid.*, p. 223.

34. Hiltner, *op cit.*, p. 101.

35. Zilboorg, *Mind, Medicine and Man*, pp. 308 f.

36. Stefan Zweig, *Die Heiling durch den Geist* (Leipzig, 1931), pp. 12 ff.

37. Henry E. Sigerist, *Antike Heilkunde* (Munich, 1927), p. 29.

38. *Ibid.*, p. 47.

39. Charles Singer and H.E. Sigerist, eds., *Essays on the History of Medicine* (Zurich, 1924), p. 198.

40. Sigerist, *Grosse Artze* (Munich, 1932), p. 103.

41. George Santayana, *Some Turns of Thought in Modern Philosophy* (New York, 1933), p. 31.

42. Zilboorg, *Mind, Medicine and Man*, p. 330.

43. *Ibid.*

44. Idem, *A History of Medical Psychology*, p. 229.

45. *Ibid.*, p. 108.

46. *Ibid.*, p. 109.

47. Idem, *Mind, Medicine and Man*, p. 12.

48. Jung, *op. cit.*, p. 301.

49. *Ibid.*, p. 3.

50. Hiltner, *op. cit.*, p. 133.

51. *Ibid.*, p. 82.

52. *Ibid.*, p. 26.

53. Zilboorg, *Mind, Medicine and Man*, p. 226.

54. *Ibid.*, p. 64.

55. *Ibid.*, p. 226.

56. *Ibid.*, p. 48.

57. *Ibid.*

The Meaning of Health

The difficulty and the challenge of this subject is that in order to speak of health, one must speak of all dimensions of life which are united in man. And no one can be an expert in all of them. But confronting this challenge is the destiny of the philosopher and the theologian, insofar as they should envisage the whole of life. In any case, only a limited part of the immense problem can be covered.

A logical consideration

The title is not "the concept of health," but "the meaning of health." Concepts are defined by subsumption to a more embracing concept; meanings are defined by being brought into configuration with other meanings. This method is in many cases more adequate and not less scientific than the method of subsumption. In our case, it is definitely adequate for a very fundamental reason. Health is not an element in the description of man's essential nature — his *eidos* or *ide*, as Plato would say; his created nature, as theology would express it. Health is not a part of man or a function of man, as are blood circulation, metabolism, hearing, breathing. Health is a meaningful term only in confrontation with its opposite — disease. And disease contains a partial negation of the essential nature of man. Conversely, in order to understand disease, one must know the essential nature of man as well as the possible distortions of it. In contemporary language one would say that health and disease are existentialist concepts. They do not grasp something of man's essential nature; certainly they presuppose this nature and the knowledge of it; but they add a new element, the possibility and reality of its distortion. Health and disease are very good examples of existentialist concepts. Like theology, medicine always did unite essentialist and existentialist elements in its thought. Therefore, psychotherapy, especially in its psychoanalytic form, and existentialism have influenced each other profoundly in the last fifty years; and the idea of an existentialist psychotherapy is only a confirmation and systematization of an actual situation.

The basic dialectics of life processes

Life processes include two basic elements: self-identity and self-alteration. A centered and balanced living whole goes beyond itself partly from its unity, but in doing so it tries to preserve its identity and to return in its separated parts to itself. Going out from one's self and returning to one's self characterizes life under all dimensions, from the structure of the atom to the growth of the plant, to the movement of the animal, to the creativity of the mind, to the dynamics of historical groups. One can call this dialectics of life processes because it implies contrasting movements, a *yes* and a *no*, as in a searching conversation. And all dialectical thought is nothing but a mirror of such life processes.

The contrast between self-identity and self-alteration produces two dangers for every living being. The first is to lose one's self in going beyond one's self and not being able to return to one's self. This happens if special processes separate themselves from the whole and produce dispersion into too many directions, a wrong kind of growth, a loss of the uniting center. In all these cases (which are represented by particular bodily and mental diseases and personal disintegrations) the self-identity is threatened and often completely lost (change of personality and memory).

In reaction to the awareness of this danger, the opposite danger appears. Afraid to lose one's identity, one is unable to go out from one's self into self-alteration. Perhaps one has attempted it, but after having been frustrated, one retreats to a limited form of existence in which the self-identity on a reduced basis is preserved; and it is not only preserved, it is compulsively defended as in most cases of psychoneurosis.

If we ask how it can be explained that the dialectics of life processes are interrupted and how its flux is stopped, we may name three main causes: accidents, intrusions, imbalances. A consideration of these would lead deeply into the philosophy of life, and especially of medicine; we can only point to some characteristics of these causes of disease, as well as to their common cause. They are rooted in what I call the ambiguity of life and of all its processes. Ambiguity means that in every creative process of life, a destructive trend is implied; in every integrating process of life, a disintegrating trend; in every process toward the sublime, a profanizing trend. These ambiguities of life produce the concrete causes of disease. The ambiguities of encounter of being with being make destructive accidents unavoidable, be it bodily injuries or psychological traumata.

The ambiguities of assimilation of elements of the surrounding world — in food, breathing, communication — make unavoidable the destructive intrusions of strange bodies, as in bodily or mental infections; the ambiguities of growth, that is, bodily growth or the development of one's spiritual potentialities, make unavoidable the appearance of imbalances. Generally speaking, disease is a symptom of the universal ambiguity of life. Life must risk itself in order to win itself, but in the risking it may lose itself. A life which does not risk disease — even in the highest forms of the life of the spirit — is a poor life, as is shown, for instance, by the hypochondriac or the conformist.

Health, disease, and healing under different dimensions of life

When I spoke of dimensions of life, there was implied a rejection of the phrase "levels of life." This must now be made explicit. Man should not be considered as a composite of several levels, such as body, soul, spirit, but as a multidimensional unity. I use the metaphor "dimension" in order to indicate that the different qualities of life in man are present within each other and do not lie alongside or above each other. One can expediently, but not necessarily, distinguish the physical, the chemical, the biological, the psychological, the mental, and the historical dimensions. Different distinctions as well as more particular ones are quite possible. What is important, however, is to see that they do not lie alongside, but within each other, as in the metaphor "dimension" the dimensional lines cross each other in one point.

This point, in our consideration, is man. He is multidimensional unity; all dimensions, distinguishable in experienced life, cross in him. In every dimension of life, all dimensions are potentially or actually present. In the atom only one of them is actual. In man all of them are actually present; he does not consist of levels of being, but he is a unity which unites all dimensions. This doctrine stands against the dualistic theory which sees man as composed of soul and body; or body and mind; or body, soul, and spirit, etc. Man is one, uniting within himself all dimensions of life — an insight which we partly owe to the recent developments of medicine, especially psychiatry.

As confirmation of this idea, one may refer to psycho-somatic medicine. But although this is not incorrect, one should not forget that a hyphen between "psycho" and "somatic" represents the statement of a problem and not a solution.

The multidimensional unity of life in man calls for a multidimensional concept of health, of disease, and of healing, but in such a way that it becomes obvious that in each dimension all the others are present.

I shall follow the series of dimensions as indicated before and in each case show the meaning of health and disease and the function of healing as determined by the ideas of health and disease in what one could call a philosophy of life in medical terms.

Mechanical dimension
Under the predominance of the physical dimension, health is the adequate functioning of all the particular parts of man. Disease is the non-functioning of these parts because of incidents, infections, and imbalances. Healing, then, is the removal of the diseased parts or their mechanical replacement: surgery. The prevalence of surgery since the Renaissance is based on an image of man (classically formulated by Descartes) which views him as a well-functioning body-machine, the disabled parts of which are removed or replaced so that after successful surgery, health means the functioning of the machine with reduced or artificially strengthened force. Analogies to bodily surgery in the other dimensions can be found, for instance, in the removal of elements in the psychological makeup of a person by psychotherapeutic methods. The patient is healed but reduced in power of being. A

conspicuous case in which bodily surgery and psychological reduction are united is lobotomy, the total being reduced to a rather low functioning, but in some respect being healed. And under the dimension of the spirit, there can also be found an analogy in the moral and educational repressing of vital trends which have become infected or imbalanced, and dangerous for the whole. But such healing of the person is surgery; its healing is reduction of the power of being.

Chemical dimension
There is no bodily surgery which does not consider the chemical processes in the body that is operated on. Health in this dimension is the balance of chemical substances and processes in a living organism. Here, reduction by sedatives and increase by adding stimulating substances to the organism are eqally important. But it is not full healing in either case. The present drug-medicine fashion puts before us a profound problem. If it is possible to determine the self-altering as well as the self-preserving life processes in a living being from the dimension of chemism, what does this mean for the dimensions of the psychological, the spiritual, and the historical? In answering this, one must realize that even if we imagined the total determination of individuals on this basis as possible, the question would remain: what about the chemism of those who determine the chemical composition of others? Who decides? Here the dimension of health in the social-historical structure — with its presuppositions of spirit, morality, culture, and religion — appears in the health idea of the "brave new world." In this idea of human health, self-alteration is reduced to a minimum and life dries up.

Biological dimension
Disregarding these extremes, which are threats on the horizon of our life, we must consider the biological dimension in which the balance is achieved between self-alteration and self-preservation. This is done by acts in which the total organism in its relation to environment and world is the object of healing, as for instance through rest, awakening of interest, increased movement, change of food and climate, etc. This is well expressed in the word "re-creation," which indicates that the created vitality was stopped

either in its power of going out beyond itself or in its power of returning to itself. Either the life processes had been reduced to routine existence or they were excited by the innumerable stimuli of daily life. Here a new dimension appears. The attempt to recreate life in the biological dimension demands the inclusion of the problem of health in the dimension of self-awareness — the psychological.

Psychological dimension
Health in the dimension of self-awareness shows the dialectical structure of life processes most clearly. The processes of psychological growth demand self-alteration in every moment, in receiving reality, in mastering it, in being united with parts of it, in changing it, etc. But in all this a risk is involved, and this accounts for the reluctance to take all these encountered pieces of reality into one's centered self; thus the desire to withdraw into a limited reality becomes effective. One is afraid of going out and one defends compulsively the limited place to which one has retired. Something went wrong in the process of pushing ahead. And now a reduced health is unconsciously produced. The reduced health of the neurotic is the limited health he is able to reach — but reality makes him aware of the dangers of his limitation and so he wants to overcome the limits with the help of the analyst. If in reaching some degree of liberation, reality shows itself to him irrefutably, the question arises whether the neurotic can face reality. Often he can, sometimes he cannot; and it is left to the judgment of the healer whether he shall even try to heal if the result is so ambiguous.

We can compare the causes of psychological diseases with the causes of bodily diseases. Traumatic experiences stand in analogy to accidents (and are sometimes caused by accidents) and are the intrusion of forces which remain alongside the centered self as strange elements which are not taken into the center. Healing means helping to make somebody aware of these inhibitions of the outgoing processes and accepting the fact of limited health, because if it is accepted, its compulsory form is undercut and openness for pushing ahead becomes possible. Then, of course, the danger arises that the outgoing process may become so uninhibited that the return is stopped and self-identity is destroyed.

Spiritual dimension

Again we are in the situation that we have separated the dimension of self-awareness from the dimension of spirit ("spirit," with a small *s* designating the life in meanings and values inherent in morality, culture, and religion). In these three functions of the spirit, the problem of health receives another depth and breadth, which then, conversely, is decisive for all the preceding dimensions. Morality is the self-actualization of the person in his centered encounter with the other person. This act is the basis of life in the dimension of the spirit. It is not the subjection to a law from God or man, but it is the actualization of what we potentially are, of our created nature. Its distortion in the line of self-identity as a person is the lawless explosion of all possibilities.

Here the psychotherapeutic problem becomes the moral problem of the person and his self-actualization. And healing is the power of overcoming both distortions. But the healing of the spirit is not possible by good will, because the good will is just that which needs healing. In order to be healed, the spirit must be grasped by something which transcends it, which is not strange to it, but within which is the fulfillment of its potentialities. It is called "Spirit" (with a capital *S*). Spirit is the presence of what concerns us ultimately, the ground of our being and meaning. This is the intention of religion, but it is not identical with religion. For as a function of the human spirit and as a realm of human activities, religion also stands under the dialectics of all life and under its ambiguities and, because its claims are higher, is even more profound than the others. Religious health is the state of being grasped by the Spirit, namely the divine presence, enabling us to transcend our religion and to return to it in the same experience. Unhealthy religion is the state of being enslaved — socially or personally — by a concrete religious system, producing bigotry, fanaticism, inordinate self-destructive ecstasy, dogmatism, ritualism. But neither is it healthy if in the breakthrough out of all this one loses the identity of a personal and communal religious center.

It must be added here that the healing power of the Spiritual Presence is far removed from the magic practice of "faith-healing." There *is* such a thing, a magic force from man to man. And without doubt the magic influence of the healer on the patient or of the patient upon himself is an element in most forms of healing. (Magic: the impact of one unconscious power upon another one.) But this is not the healing power of being centered in the universal, the divine center.

Here again the question arises how the healing helper, in most cases the minister or priest, can judge (like the psychoanalyst) whether the self-restriction to a religion of limited health (accepting authority, relying on a conversion experience) should be accepted or revealed in its limitation; and the same in a well-established remoteness from a concrete religion. When is conversion required for Spiritual health?

Historical dimension
When dealing with the cultural function in the light of the idea of health, we are driven to the last of the dimensions of life, the historical. The decisive question here is: To what degree is personal health possible in a society which is not a "sane society" (Erich Fromm)? "By creating a sane society" is an inadequate answer: first, because it disregards the ambiguities of historical existence which can be conquered only fragmentarily; second, because it overlooks the fact that without personal health in the leading groups, no social health is possible (the communist society). The cultural situation of a society has the same dialectics — the inhibition against pushing forward or the impossibility of returning to a guiding set of symbols. The unsolved situation in this respect is partly the result, partly the cause of the lack of health in all the other dimensions. But this goes beyond our limited subject.

Healing, separated and united

The road through the many dimensions, and the meaning of health within them, has shown, first, that the dialectics of life processes are the same under each dimension; second, that in each of them the others are presupposed; third, that there is always a fulfilling and a reducing idea of health; fourth, that complete healing includes healing under all dimensions.

This raises the question of the justification of limited healing.

Human finitude makes particular healing necessary. The hurt finger requires surgical or chemical help, the physically healthy neurotic requires psychotherapeutic help. There are special helpers and healing methods called for under every dimension. But this independence of particular ideas of health and healing is limited by the mutual within-each-otherness of the dimensions. This is partly untrue to the human situation and leads to a phenomenon I would call "unhealthy health." It comes about if healing under one dimension is successful but does not take into consideration the other dimensions in which health is lacking or even imperilled by the particular healing. Successful surgery may produce a psychological trauma; effective drugs may calm down an uneasy conscience and preserve a moral deficiency; the well-trained, athletic body may contain a neurotic personality; the healed patient of the analyst may be sick through a lack of an ultimate meaning of his life; the conformist's average life may be sick through inhibited self-alteration; the converted Christian may suffer under repressions which produce fanaticism and may explode in lawless forms; the sane society may be the place where the pressure of the principles of its sanity may produce psychological and biological disruptions by the desire for creative insanity.

Particular healing is unavoidable, but it has the tendency to provoke diseases in another realm.

Thus, it is important for healers always to cooperate in every healing situation. This requirement was embodied in the ideal of the *soter*, the saviour (precisely, "the healer") who makes healthy and whole. The word has been applied to medical men, to gods of healing, to great rulers, to divine-human mediators. They all were considered to be healers. But the ideal was the *one* healer, the saviour, whose healing powers indicate the coming of the new eon. This is the background of the New Testament accounts of healing, which should not be taken as miracle stories, but as stories pointing to the universal healer.

This mythological symbol, which was applied to the man Jesus, shows the unity of the religious and the medical most clearly. And if salvation is understood in the sense of healing, there is no conflict between the religious and the medical, but the most intimate relation. Only a theology which has forgotten this relation, and sees salvation as the elevation of the individual to a heavenly place, can come into conflict with medicine. And only a medicine which denies the non-biological dimensions of life in their significance for the biological dimension (including its physical and chemical conditions) can come into conflict with theology. But an understanding of the differences as well as the mutual within-each-otherness of the dimensions can remove the conflict and create an intensive collaboration of helpers in all dimensions of health and healing.

The concept of health cannot be defined without relation to its opposite — disease. But this is not only a matter of definition. In reality, health is not health without the essential possibility and the existential reality of disease. In this sense, health is disease conquered, as eternally the positive is positive by conquering the negative. This is the deepest theological significance of medicine.

Acknowledgements

"The Relation of Religion and Health" first appeared in the RE-VIEW OF RELIGION, Columbia University Press.
"The Meaning of Health" first appeared in PERSPECTIVES OF BIOLOGY AND MEDICINE. Permission to publish these two essays granted by Dr. Robert Kimball is gratefully acknowledged.

Typographic design by Jack W. Stauffacher of the Greenwood Press, San Francisco California. Set in Sabon and Janson-Antiqua types.

Cover illustration : ASCLEPIUS (Asklepios), Graeco-Roman, bronze, first century B. C. or first century A. D. Courtesy of the Museum of Fine Arts, Boston, Masachusetts.